Other Books by Laura Jensen

AFTER I HAVE VOTED (1972)

ANXIETY AND ASHES (1976)

BAD BOATS (1977)

TAPWATER (1978)

THE STORY MAKES THEM WHOLE (1979)

MEMORY (1982)

A SKY EMPTY OF ORION (1985)

Shelter

SHELTER

by

Laura Jensen

Dragon Gate, Inc.

Port Townsend, Washington

Grateful acknowledgment is made to the following publications in which some of these poems first appeared: *American Poetry Review*, "Sunburned Woman"; *Field*, "Dull Brown," "Crowsong," "George," "Adoration of the Anchor," "Pinks," "Lessons," "Dull Winter," "Child,"; *Ironwood*, "While the Cherry Tree Is Flowering"; *Mid-American Review*, "World without Poison"; *The Montana Review*, "Snail to Swallow" and "Mended Boots"; *Poet & Critic*, "Untitled" (retitled "Searching") and "Like Swallows at the Pilings of the Ferry"; *The Poetry Miscellany*, "Calling," "I Have a Fondness for the Truth," "Child Hiding"; *Poetry Northwest*, "Window Views"; *Seattle Review*, "I'll Make You a Cat" and "Destinations."

Some of the poems in *Shelter* appeared previously in a chapbook from Meadow Press entitled *A Sky Empty of Orion* (1985).

The author would like to thank the Ingram Merrill Foundation for a grant that greatly aided her in completing *Shelter*.

Both the author and the publisher wish to express their gratitude to the Literature Program of the National Endowment for the Arts for a grant that helped support the publication of this book.

Dragon Gate, Inc., 508 Lincoln Street
Port Townsend, Washington 98368

Cover art is from a watercolor painting, "Crows' Conversation," by Linda Okazaki in the collection of the Spokane School District, purchased under the Washington State Art in Public Places Program.

Library of Congress Cataloging in Publication Data

Jensen, Laura, 1948-
Shelter.

I. Title.
PS3560.E59S4   1985   811'.54   85-12861
ISBN 0-937872-28-8
ISBN 0-937872-29-6 (pbk.)

Contents

III

IV

V

I

The Storm

In the room with the bed
there has not been a dream
where your heart is screaming
let me wake, let me wake.
At the windows are trees.
At the windows are swallows.
On the table are books.
On the table are candles.
Each little room is clean,
and at the door are pansies.
And a rosebush down the stairs.

The landlord gave me jasmine
in earth from the ladder
when he rebuilt the stair.
I water the jasmine.
The landlord climbs the stair.
Now he asks me to carry
the plants indoors. I lift them
to newsprint on the table
over the clean kitchen floor.

Clouds darken the weather.
The wind chimes shake and flail.
In slicker and sou'wester
on breaking crests the landlord
storms the paint from the walls
with a pressurized jet,
and turns the world over.
A snowstorm surrounds
the house in a glass ball,
my face at the window.
I think winter is here.

Window Views

EGRET WINDOW

1.

Move about on a train.
The purse must not swing.
Make a fist near a handhold,
a railing.

Water birds float or pass over
the dawn, clear and controlled.
After Oakland
the faces are progressively
more strange, red as sunrise,
their sun yet rising,
not yet morning, not midmorning,
a church painted cream.

And after Merced
the cattle are for once
doing what is appropriate,
standing humbly
in the cream-colored grass,
under the clean sky.
The half-grown calf stands nearby
its mother, keeps its head
against her side.

2.

Egret be what we see through,
the white fog blessedly making
the ash tree forget its surroundings.

All that is beautiful
hangs on a thread that is tied to a nail
in Christ's palm,
the thread frail as spider web,
the nail of iron . . .

That is day starting, day says
hammer, clang at a pipe.

Be there no human here,
be there here the flat marsh
before man, be there here

those bony wings,
arching, convoluting
powerful illogical opening
as the white wings
startle with size at their spread.

ROBIN WINDOW

The nearly new
would put their faces
near your eye. It looks

like licorice and sees
while you eat the berries
that have been in damp fog
for days.

What could muffle
a twig that creaks on glass
while you ride?

7

Children alone in houses
call the curtain the whole world
harm does not see through

or call the world the curtain
hiding their harm.

Redbreast, the lacy flock of you
presses a shadow into the carpet.

EARTHQUAKE WINDOW

How do you see the stars light up
along the branch of the landlord's ash tree?
Is it enough to elicit faith in astrology?
It rains and the sky is a certain shade.

Can you see any farther than the ash tree?
Can you see any farther past you than the rain?

She says it is mice that bump in the wall.
It could be bricks crumbling under earthquake.

The way the house here rocks is like a boat
in a wash, while mind just remains, riding,
riding the earthquake, talking along the line.

Only an earthquake. For what is the night
more made of than uncertainty, even more uncertain
without the earth quaking, echoing oddly
the state of mind.

OWL WINDOW

What joy to count to three, to think of three
things at one time. To think of yesterday,

some sparrows flying: suddenly they think,
they are not angry that they cannot fly if only
they can see us flying. Suddenly one thinks,
they are not angry that they cannot fly if only
they can look at the pattern of feathers on my wing.

To think of one dream, the dream of a house that is
low to the ground, where one woman lives, and the house
is on the other side of a pasture. In the pasture
are many dark ponies, and the woman walks on the road
in dim moonlight, hearing the hooves of the ponies
pounding with great delicacy along the sod.

And to think of the second part of the dream
where another woman lives in a room in a house
in dim darkness, and at the window a pliant owl,
all eyes, all eyes and patterned feathers.

What joy to count to three, to think of three
things at one time and have no fear, no fear at all.

MOON WINDOW

What is it like to dream?
What is it like to live alone, to cover
everything, then cross your arm over arm
and say, later, tomorrow, when I am warm,
the moon will be the cameo far from the trees:

for the night is an old black sweater, where
you put your eye to the heart of Breasted-One,
you see her pin as you weep.

GOODBYE

old house with the yellow
windows. She packs
and steps out into snow.
Her eyes follow
a woman's little opera glasses
up to the treetop. The woman
draws back into her home.

Running away, then.

At the laundromat
she reads no allegiance
into the clothes
of a woman pounding
on the office door for restitution.
Nothing shallow,
she washes all
her flannel nightwear

in the snow. Something
this white, why ask
where it comes from?
From the only snow of the year,
this white water must last her.

I am crazy, she thinks. I am
crazy, crazy like a fox.

Dull Winter

Could you hear
fire from water, smoke from fog,
gravel from leaves underfoot?

See
a pine tree with
a stubby top
from a slipper?

Could you tell cottonwood
leaves in the cup from tea?

Is the moon in the tree
where the sun was,
and the wind in the leaves
like someone on the porch?

Did you know, Kublai Khan
rushed down to the sea
of Japan, and the vessels

sank there to the slugs
and plumes to be treasure?
In what language
did this not occur?

Dull Brown

"Easy to Be Hard"
—THREE DOG NIGHT

Hard to wish
the fragments of the jam jars
cleared of their spattered shadows,
and the sky again naïve
or at least blasé or calm with buds,
the dishes and teacups
set numerous and numinous
on whole mats and whole saucers,
and all the china dolls
offered back their small fingers,
offered back their hollow skulls.

Easier when a bird flies by
and flies by smug because
it builds a nest out of nothing
and builds a shell out of love,
the love that pecks away at hearts
chip, chip, so mindlessly to itself,
the love with its gliding experience.

But when I step out I begin to sob.

Hard to wish
for the wings of an angel, easy
to wish for the wings of a bird
when they are and I am not and it is
so hard to be human, so hard.

I flew once, with a lot of help,
over Saginaw, Michigan. As oars

feather water, so snow was feathered
by wind over fields of Saginaw,
and up rose from large farmhouses
a feeling like kitchens of bread.
Nothing so flat and brown and dull
could be heartless. Of Saginaw,
that is all I know. Only that
and the sight of some sound fences.

There's the same dull brown
on the best wing, on the best trunk
of a tree.

Child,

During the great and humorless invisible winter,
none of the loaves would mold, the air stayed
shiftless, and great dark smears appeared
on the linoleum below the sink, under the witless
broom, under the Frigidaire door where sometimes
a little juice spilled or some new ice was made.
The winter was a boot track. Or a fly that never knew
life would not go on like that.
                                    Buds were invisible
inside the trees. Every blossom on the cherry tree
was invisible. Invisible rocks sat unseeable
on tables. Shells at the beach were too far away
to believe.
                    Invisible lawn mowers in garages smelled
dull, like oil, and had no significance. Invisible
sunlight scented the clouds and had no meaning.

During the great uninteresting gray and invisible
winter you forgot about flowers and enough to eat,
about everything but the flat dull house and the
flat dull hours and the invisible landlord's heel.
You forgot the sun, and the renewal of grass.
You forgot friends. Now forget the terrible
unpleasant, unforgivable, humorless invisible winter.
Let it drift out on the air when you open the kitchen
door, just as they say, and hope it goes away.

Two Stripes

What we took to be God, the light,
floated through the dark in candles
carried in the free hands of couples.
These cars looked so holy
light-years away from bus riders
in their lighted spots, they wondered
if cars were not really love.
The rain was so dark
there was nothing but stream to it,
candles in water under bridges.

A turn of the knob lets night in,
lets in the first clangs and horns of
the year, and through both doors.

Small striped snails crossed to earth
over sidewalk, then broke at the roots
of shrubs, shreds of ornament.
One sleek, small ball is blue as a shiny
blue truck cab with the back piled high
with snowy firewood. Within that blue

a room reflects.

The snow entered the space
between whatever it could not penetrate,
it snowed and I walked out
down the white and brush-beside road,
found a bird had signed its name there,
written *Two Stripes! I am Two Stripes!*
then flown. This I will remember,
if someone remembers my circling,
puzzled boot tracks.

Port Orford Cedars

Their greens in suspension are a heavy fringe
in shadow but the opposite
is a roof made of tile. In bad weather
rain beads and runs in a stream.

Some trickles at the fringe, but a whole river
extends the mystery of cedar.
How rain reaches the farthest roots
but at the center is a heart as dry as bone.

In the sunlight it is surface like any fabric,
it is the touch where you handle it—
more poignant when you are hungry, more terrible
when you are far away from home.

Record Store

The trunks of the trees are thick, black, wet.
The ground is luminous with leaves. The leaves
made wine. On the ground was a string of green
glass beads. No face makes a haven like these.

The autumn soaks my clothes, the squabbling
jays have vanished with the blossoms, the cedar
waxwings in their imperfect plumage
took the berries from the hawthorn and flew.

No face makes a haven like yours in the dark
as the rain makes the day a dark thing.
I sit beneath hookahs hearing you make change.
The arm passes over a turntable and the same

song begins. In the afternoon dark the neon
bleeds, drinks fill the glasses, and smoke
clouds the hookahs in softly lit houses
and rain is welcome, softening, softening.

Cats That Are Not Mine,
In Black and White

The cat cries something
in her sleep, a laughing
cry I cannot understand.

Whenever we sleep
we want to feel the way
a cat appears to feel
whenever it sleeps.

The black cat saw me
home with stalks of weed,
tailed me five blocks
to the store, kept me
in sight with his head
around the door.
And Blanca followed me
when it was bleak.
I ran from her domestic scene.
Cream cat buzzing in my lap.
Small white insanity
(I said to her)
I am not so very wild
that I do not want something
on a hot steamy theme
with a cookie. Coffee
at four for solitary
people. Slow tap
of the rain.

When the dog barks
with the whole dog
may the tree have
a whole cat up it.

Crowsong

One dropped a love note
from the sky to the road
so I rushed out
for the billet-doux:
butcher paper
from 37 cents worth of pickle loaf.

When I handed the postman
my book of poems
there was nothing. Later
while fluffs of late fat snow
hurried through sunlight
crows looked in from the branch.
We want to eat your eyes,
they thought, *when you are dead.*

He crosses the water
with shadow, dips in
and swims, comes up blacker
than ever, and he wants more.
So he hides in the pine
among the pale splash
of the needles
and croons of the bubble
he found there.
Once one crow finds a pearl
in an oyster it chuckles
underwater forever more.

That crow knows we watch
as he dodges on the chimney top.
He wants the coals
that should glow down there,
the shiny red coals. He wants.

I Want Some

After a week I lift the shades
and see it in Cinemascope.

I am in the front row.

(The one time that happened, my neck
hurt all evening, my child eyes blurred
with the gloss of the roans and the red
Mounties' coats.) It is so far

to this world where a tree
of camellias stands in the sunlight
at the porch of the abandoned house
where a glassless window
is propped open to ventilate.

And though the air floats around
where no one can poke a head out an
upstairs window and shake down a mop
and say, no!

I will not steal some.

I have stood
so many times just down the street
and peered
to where a bus should return
like a stone you dropped from a bridge
coming back at you, that I feel I know

this poor lost house—
that developed tilt, that air
of studied mystery, that appeal.

But I will not steal some
before I stand and wait.

I want some.
Oh, how I do.

I I

Organisms in Which the Blooms Fade Away

We stood at the window.
The moon was up but he would not look for it.
He might well have said it. It's nothing.
Nothing? The moon?

Once I followed confused through a meadow, walked
where he walked. No bird in the sky, we were in it.
No jet crossing water and stone from the mind.
They continued to bloom there, ugly husk flowers,
losses and debts. The sun that maintained them
was wasting its strength and its time. Rough
weeds were so high I could follow no deeper. An edge
of sweet trees was all I could enter. I stayed
in the light, where sorrow ends a moment,
but never really ends, a sorrow in his eyes.

He loves me, he loves me not. We are like that,
tremulous heads that droop in the sunlight
and flower in the heart, and wrench stillness away.
Recollect what we want, a flower in the arm,
this flower, this tug. Good times are slowly gone,
organisms in which the blooms fade away.

Army Jets

I walked out in the pale winter sun.
They fly over the edge of the district,
always with the belly open.
They could see the whole area,
small blocks with trees, my white face
turned up from my striped hood.

They could play their war games in an empty
city, run up the back steps of my small
apartment, burst in with one boot
and demand the Spam. Then site out the window
while I cower at a wall, waving my small
paper flag.

The moon
comes so seldom to the window. But it came
this evening full and shocked with white,
looked in the space between the woodwork
and the edge of the window shade.

I wanted it to stay, squinted to cover
the walls with its rays. The room was a pale
and listless chilly shadow.
Later I woke to remember the army jets,
autumn and winter, always low and with thunder,
gun-gray metal objects falling slowly,
too big to be dreams across the moist gray sky.

At the Travel Agency

And Earth,
that is the Earth down there,
the tear-streaked granite face
of the mountains in winter,
the Mississippi River that snakes,
the odd circular grooves
of irrigation.

This is Earth too—
the glass and steel view
from the travel agency window. Souvenirs
tilt on the desk of the agent.
She is the agent of what stretches a cable
over the world. Where a metal sheet
shakes in the wings to sham a thunder
on the face of the genuine Earth.

When I heard the thunder as a child
and saw the low belly of the heavy
dark and gray propeller-driven stone,
I would run to the garage and hide me there,
near the spades and rakes and gritty
oil-smelling rucksacks with the few
canned provisions toward emergency,
and the same when the air raid
siren blared. I was scared.

If you want to imagine,
to suppose toward an Earth
our places pocked
where the bombs scalded, say:
We are working on coming partway.

Once pine and fir grew,
once a doe ran through salal
and fern and berry, where double-
lane intersections and these twelve-story
old-time buildings clutter Earth today.

Mended Boots

She drops the ticket into the box
and says it's lost. Our heads
nearly touch over the top as we peer
in there, where a few green stubs
are scattered. It's the stunned stump
of a month called January, in the store
women lean their backs at the other
counter while they count.

The boots come out unfamiliar.
The air in the shoe repair is like
no other. She breathes what she has to.

Separate

And it went on and on,
not a dream, not a dance,
like a long, planned chance encounter.

The world watched,
not as it watches the bread rise,
not as it watches the lock
as it locks up at night,

but as it sees something else
when a gull drifts
motionless past the window.
Not even the word *gull*
enters the mind.

When the world came between
it was not planned. The way
a car covers the sidewalk,
part of its driveway. For a long time
she had thought that it was love,
then she thought that she knew something—

but she had to be silent about it.
She knew there were
prisons, and crazyhouses.

She also thought
she saw the gull, flying home at dusk.
But it flew behind a building
and was hidden from her view.

Sunburned Woman

She does not know how far the earth
is from the sun or how far each
of its small stones, or what their names,
or what to count to to count them.
They are like dwarves each with a bed
a girl tucks them up in at night
and sings and sings
                                    and then grows up.
But night is when there is no sun
but the red holes that glow from backs,
their slight broad fat crossed white with straps
and the mute force
                            of grains of sand
left in sand pails. Fire on the edge
of a pine woods as it walks through
each tree, then through two trees as though
each cross were nailed one to one more
like a truth. It does not grow mad.
But it takes what stands too still
in its hands, which have no distance
and no number, like her heart now
which does not know
                                    but reaches out.
It does not stay in her arms long.
It does not stay in their arms long.
The ones the trees put around her.

But when she puts black dirt in pots
it makes her round. She takes on shadow
and dimension. It is an odd
sort of worship but all she knows —

the sun   the earth   the woman   and
a star she sees just above her.

The rooms can make her round they make
her walk from one to the other.
When it goes down she can go out
just by holding her hand around
a candleflame. She blows it out.

She does not know all the colors
of the spectrum or their order.
She does not know
                    even paint box,
but that one shrunk, then vanished.
But which
                    was gone fast, like its name?

Japanese Prints

Rain this morning. At the museum I studied
the representation of fabric in the clothing in
the Japanese prints.
A flower on a circle circled
by more petals, gold bands interlaced and broad tear-
drops like moons inside the bands.
A peach-
colored facing at the neck of a courtesan.
Kimono,
pale ground where fruit branch and blossom are whole.

Kimono, a black ground with white clouds
where pines are spread.
Actresses, hands concealed
deep in deep sleeves, their teeth seed pearls. Roles
scribed on the paper under glass.

But in the winter rain small people
bent over as they walked. Their clothes were tan.
They hurried through the street in the distance.
No fruit trees blossomed on their backs.

At home the rain stopped. In the dark I remembered
when I was a girl I sewed myself a dress, a long
dress of black cotton cloth scattered with roses,
sleeves like a kimono.

I shut the door slowly, not there, not yet gone
away from within the thick walls where you are.
In June sun, how easy to rise up and walk.
I picked up my bones that hang like fools forever

by the road in the winter wind, flesh blowing off
without your thick walls.
And I felt like that girl,
crazy as a loon and powerfully glad of it, in my
kimono in my mother's garden filled with chrysanthemums.

Stigmata

The ruby throats of the doves
do not astound you. All the people
have a spot on them, a cluster

of cherries at the mouth,
a cowlick your mother
brushed around and never

could tame down, until it became
chronic and reminded her
underneath your hat of a stain

at the hem of the blouse
she kept tucked in.
You should know where you're going.

You should have the flower
you came all this way to see
clutched in your hand.

Snail to Swallow

takes thought. You've always got
to remember he can't tell that's not
wing-weight loading down his foot
and the effortless god-making of the grass
he becomes center of as he forces the green
to radiate, the halo-becoming deifying
what is becoming is not ever what he is
thinking about. And as he sees the sky
as without any substance, as unseeable
to his unexisting eye, nothing tells him,
or me, that the swallow is part of his light
shining from him, from the center of his
spiral, which turns without thinking
begin. Or end. Or not.

Six Dreams

THE DOVES

The house is an enormous house.
It has one parakeet, one cage.
I come in. There is one bee in one corner.
I open the door and it does not fly out.
In flies another. I put down a jar
and capture them both, together.

And they are two boneless doves,
fat boneless chicken in a jar.
When I hold them up to the light
at the door away they fly.
Bones and wings and feathers flutter.

CHRISTMAS

The house is an enormous house.
It is Christmas, and he wanders around.
I wander. It is dark inside, and it is dark out.
I walk out on the road, with several people.
We are caught by a murderer.
Talking with the women, I raise my arms
in a gesture. My undershirt rises over my breasts.
We leave the murderer, he has grown old,
a dark-haired man in a business suit,
attended by his chauffeur.
I see the moon. The moon is enormous,
antique and cracked and mottled,
the color of an orange.

THE OCEAN

The ocean is enormous.
I will settle my life in a sum,
a little problem in arithmetic.
He shows me the waves.
The ocean is enormous,
one enormous problem
that is overpowering.

THE IMAGES

I walk in the snow by moving trains.
My good friend is with me.
She uses wooden images
for a traveling show, they are just down the line
in a boxcar. They are like wood, they are
like leather, with stitches like sewn leather.
Now it is dark. And as the lights shine
from the windows of the passing trains
the images are dancing.

THE YOUNG MAN

The young man is a sensitive.
He is riding in a car, once, long ago
with his young mother.
She had bought him a coat, of fur-
lined leather. He wore it.

From the clothes of love, he grew a plant.
From his love's bikini he grew white roses.
A row of small dark girls sit on the gym floor.
Their legs stick out in front of them.
Their toe shoes are small, they are tucked
and stitched and scuffed on the bottoms.

He draws them there, looking out
from luminous eyes.

THE SEASONS

The frozen lands are enormous.
I fly over the frozen lands.
There is danger, mortal danger.
I am fond of the older man.
We try to preserve us from the enemy.
Winter is nearly over.

I go to the doctor.
There is a table in the room.
The room is enormous.
The doctor is in the other room
behind a one-way mirror.
When he looks at me his face
becomes older and dark with anger.
Outside it is raining. My gloves
lie soaking on the ground.
Spring is nearly over.
Summer comes suddenly. The trees
are very green. The older man sits

and sucks on his pipe. He looks
a long distance, to the roof
of my parents' garage. A woodpecker,
a rabbit, do repellent things there.
But the trees are still green. The sun
does not stop shining.

Searching for a Silver Ring
And Finding It in the Bedclothes

She had the flats the folds the map
and ran her hands over like water.
Newspapers from the laundromat
rattled onto the floor and settled.
Like rabbits painted in a saucer
her hands ran searching for a beach.

A silver ring is a bank of beach.
Is sunlight on glass, a spangled map.
Like rabbits-round-a-saucer
a pair of birds flew past to water
to some tree where they might settle.
Her sheets in the sun, a pile of laundry.

She searched the sheets from the laundromat
counted the birds on the beach.
Searched the papers that folded and settled.
The hot light burned on the map.
She counted the spots of milk or water
searched the tablecloth under the saucer.

And the rabbits ran blind in the saucer.
And no one did laundry at the laundromat.
There was no blue and silver water.
The pair of birds had flown from the beach.
The roads had vanished from the map
and the road dust would not settle.

She said words, birds flying and settling.
She said words about rabbits in a saucer
that never left the edge of their map.
She folded the map like the laundry
like a big towel at the beach.
And in her sleep she said words about water

said she could fall from the edge of water
hover, become a bird and settle.
Said she could drive out onto a beach
where rabbits leaped out of the saucer.
Like a tub overflowing at the laundromat
she left the edge of the map.

Then the ring in the map of the sheets. Water
made the feathers settle, did the laundry
in the saucer. A ring is a starry beach.

Butterflies

Embrace a tree in the snow.
To the tree say nothing, then.

Say to the cherry as the rain
falls down, I want to die before
your blossoms fall to the ground.
For this is a brutal world.
Say this to the cherry.

Say to the hawthorn
out the window as the blind
goes up at dawn life is sorry.
It is sorry that it uses,
that it makes no return.
Say this to the hawthorn.

Say to the roses
at the foot of the stair
I will never cut you.

When butterflies dance
in the light at the window
we say our sun is also yellow.

And when gulls fly over
in darkening blue of the sky
we say to them, I know you.
You are on your way home.

Lie in his arms in the day.
Lie in his arms in the night.
Say it is time to go home.
At the door say, there
is the moon. There is a star.

III

Calling

This world calls like a mother
to come downstairs from your dreaming.
She sets you to some task.

But it rains.
And the world never stopped the rain
for a minute.

Did she ever set you hanging
the laundry on the line
from the corner of the house
to the mast in the blackberries
and have the rain make you
take it all back, white sheet
by white sheet, and blouse by blouse?

Come down, come down and stop your dreaming.
The house grew old as I grew old
and has turned into a waiting.

I have gone back time after time,
and I have gone back crying. He says
I am like laundry at her door.
A suitcase full of troubles.

We do it at the laundromat.
And I live in a sea of tears.

I Want to Walk Out

I want to walk out but there is nowhere.
How do we walk out into the evening,
rubble through rubble, turned into stone
by the snakes inside our heads? Who would become
another stone, or become stone again?
And what of tomorrow?

I cannot turn to him again, he has nothing
to tell me, nothing to show me. He turns
to me now that his own house
is in turmoil. I want to walk out
into rubble and turn over stones.

What is it? What is this fear that remembers?
He turned me over like stone.
Now I stare silently into my empty cup.
Think of a walking out he made to find me,
to turn me over like stone and go.
And what is the use of it?

It is a wandering, being a wanderer,
being a sought thing, then a seeker,
then alone. I want to go out and search
for a wave to draw, and for words.
For stones to turn over as I did when I was younger.

On the desert a friend showed ants to her daughter.
I want to walk out there and turn over stones.
I want to see those two do this again. To turn
over stones as I did when I was younger.

This Photograph

for Janet Ness

Cherry blossoms in intermittent rain.
You photograph me by some. It is
a rental tree. They are rental cherries.

I told you when we left
that we would have to walk back up, that I
would be complaining
and puffing all the way, like a heavy woman
in a tightly laced old corset. We walk down
to the waterfront anyway. It is Sunday.
You photograph Bing Crosby's birthplace.
Plaques at the site of the first hospital,
at the site of the first school. I tell you

I am off prescription drugs forever, but am
sure I am acting irrationally, cannot count
or remember. I cannot count how many frames.

This is where my grandfather had his saloon,
I think, on the corner of Starr. I do not know
whether he owned it or drank there. I rephrase
that as we walk to a fence by a stump.
He was a fisherman and saloonkeeper.

In the water the festival boats pitch by,
speckled or laden with daffodils. You study
some through the zoom lens, you snap me there.

I cannot smell the salt. The snowless air
has smelled like ice cold melting snow all winter.

We watch the sky from the corner doorway
which might have been grandfather's saloon.
The clouds are heavy and on the move,
they shimmer in heavy contrast, but mostly
they rain. We hide underneath a tree.

I am puffing and crabbing, my glasses
are spotted and my heart is racing. I know
you do not worry about my health. Your back
hurts you now, especially when you stand still.

Should I ever want to hurt myself
to keep my tongue from slashing
some poor heart for keeps, there is walking,
walking uphill.

While the Cherry Tree Is Flowering

"Hennenberg's sister had no child. At the
death camp, she found she could choose to
stay alive, or to pick up a child and hold it
while they were gassed. She picked up
the child."

—PBS DOCUMENTARY

Floating cloud, Kwan Yin, she is the woman,
merciful Kwan Yin, momentary
as the flowering cherry, too luminous
to be hidden by the dark, too fragrant
to be forgotten.
                Mercy appears. My sister.
When her lips open a match flares
and smoke enters. Mercy cannot live forever.
                She has not spoken.
                Mercy can listen.
                Mercy is
momentary, sister, momentary
as the flowering cherry.

Mercy is Cannonball Adderly. "Sometimes
we're not prepared for adversity." Mercy is
"Mercy, Mercy, Mercy."

She rises and falls with the weather.
What is the music the trombone is making.
What are the words the man is saying.

Remember. Remember. European Mercy
kept her hands together, kept her lips
together and kissed the rail. Mercy

was seldom there.

Floating cloud, flowering cherry.
Do not listen to me
about the mercy of the sister of Hennenberg.
Hear him, hear him tell the story
of his sister's mercy.

She is the woman. She is the floating cloud.

I cannot bear to tell you
the story of her mercy.

Hear Hennenberg while the cherry tree is flowering.
Too luminous to be hidden by the dark.
Too fragrant to be forgotten.

Searching

Although I am very tired,
I am not as tired as a man,
nor as tired as my old mother,
nor as tired as God with the way
we are working. How white my mind
at this pointless looking
down at rocks and weeds and shells.
I can turn back now.

A gull lifts up off a rock, the wave
curls in like a seashell, a sail
makes a solid spot where the eye can rest.
Where are you now? I cannot find you anywhere.

Where I am not, do you look for me?
Where I was for a year, once in a while
you found me. Why pass your hand
over my doorknob? Why walk up the back stair?
A spider spun what he wanted over my footstep,
it was gone before you could tear it.
Now will you knock through empty air?

That is where I was, and am not now.
But where are you? I cannot find you anywhere.

I do not know where my heart knocks.
My head opens up to the sky.
My hand opens up like a saucer
that waits around for a cup,
but does not know why.

As I Lay Down Too Tired to Believe

As I lay down too tired to believe
I thought I saw before me a woman
on an empty stage, who had to dance alone
and wear nothing. She danced for a long time
and she was clumsy. She put on bra and panties
and she danced. But the dancing
was pulling her down to the floor—
to the white floor of the white stage.
On the white floor she lay dying.

       The mushroom cloud
that was her spirit drifted out of her
and floated on the air unhealthy
and it floated and it grew and came down to me.
She floated down to me where I lay down,
and she touched me on the shoulder,
and she told somebody I was dying. But I
could look up. And she said I was pretending.
I could say nothing to her. Could mention
nothing. Not tears nor confusion nor cruelty
nor hatred nor love.

George

He is as huge and as dreadful and as green
as he has ever been. He is some color
like coppery steel, his eyes some color
that is like gold, a wise metallic alloy
of an animal that moves like light in grass.
The world is fine and smooth and clean and he
is being stroked and stroked. The pure perfection
of the turning world is as fine as it has

ever been and then he is held and it is not
the same and he kicks. He struggles and he
wants to jump but she has cut the pantaloons
away from him and groomed and petted him
and made him well before and now some clear
cold drop is forming a tear within
one eye. And he kicks at her and he would
get away. I sense it burning him. I sense

that he will never see again and so does he.
But she would never do that to him. Never.
He is dropped down and fast as grass he glides
to the door to look up at a square of light
that is the screen, and yes, he can still see.
The world, it would appear, is a dreadful place.
Later he slips out and returns in hours,
about sunset, grass scattered through his fur.

I'll Make You a Cat

I'll make you a cat, she says, first
the batter here and then the batter there, then
its feet and then its long tail. It's a cat
and you eat it up. I'll make you a horse,
she says, first the batter here, and then the batter
there, and then its legs and then its long tail.
It's a horse and you eat it up.

I'll make you a bird, she says, first
the paper folded here, then the paper
folded there, then the paper bent. Then
it's done. It's a bird and you hold it
in your hand. I'll make you a fish, she says,
first the paper folded here, then the paper
folded there, then the paper bent. Then
it's done. It's a fish and you hold it in your hand.

I'll make you a bird, she says, first
an emptiness here, then an emptiness there,
then a breath in there. It's a bird and you
hear it sing. I'll make you a horse, she says,
first an emptiness here, then an emptiness
there, then a flat place, then a hand.
It's a horse and you hear it run.

I'll make you a fish, she says, first
the wrist bent down and then the wrist bent
back and then the fingers wave. It's a fish
and you see it in the water. I'll make you
a bird she says, first the wrist bent down
then the wrist bent up and then the fingers
flutter. It's a bird and you see it fly
through the air.

I'll make you a bird, he says, first
thumbs together, then fingers spread, hold them
in lamplight. It's a bird and you see
its shadow. I'll make you a dog, he says, first
your thumb up, then fingers separating there,
in the middle, move them in lamplight.
It's a dog and you see its shadow. Now think

of Plato, now think of lamplight in an old
cave, now think of a quarrel, now watch
a shadow up to your bed. And sleep, child.

Adoration of the Anchor

She hopes to hear a word from her.
A short small word to make her be
alone in a more deserving way.
Never to make the sun come up
the sky more rose, or fewer clouds
to turn to wisps in truer sky,
but after that—the summer day—
she hopes to hear a word on that.
She turns a box of buttons, white,
and bone, green, yellow, red, and
ivory, one like a blackberry,
one like a flower, and up comes
an anchor, raised blue on white ground.
It came from nowhere. She adores
the anchor where she sits, in a
sewing corner, in her small chair.
A light at the window splashes
where the lawn sprinkler washes.
A wave of real hope colored blue
rolls over her where she adores
the anchor, then lowers it down
back into the sea whence it came.
She looks around. Home is the same.

World without Poison

We swam in the city pool enclosed
by chain-link fencing. Across a field of grass
like a meadow, under trees my mother
would read a novel like the heroine's duenna
in an ancient wood and canvas lawn sling.

In my damp skin and clothes growing
damp I walked across the sunny place
like a meadow, where under the trees
my mother sat reading like a tree herself
in an oasis. I saw a snake, a small
ribboning thing like falling from hair
and reached down without thought. It bit
with no sting, then rippled off as though
embarrassed. I looked at my hand
where two small punctures were beading.

Under the trees where my mother had been reading
I showed my hand. She showed no alarm.
East of the mountains she had seen one coiled
and nearly stepped on its diamonds.
But here there is no fear, nothing
to be afraid of.

Just so. We live without fear
of any poison. I sat so two years back
at this green table, green trees outside, reading
of Crete. Of their tables round and patterned
with grooves and hollows, where the Cretan
uncles, aunts, and great-grand-dams
twine up the sides to drink milk from bowls.

This table is partial to what is straight.
There the lines between points follow

each one after the other in their own
short distance to cross a meadow.

At the table now dust.
At the sidewalk weeds and moss sprout
in their struggle to be meadow, to be crossed.
But through the trees, in the sunlight, circles
fight away from circles. They miss; they over-
reach, they are interrupted. As even our own
benign snakes always knew.

I V

I Have a Fondness for the Truth

In the early morning I heard hoofbeats,
hurried to the window from the bed
to see a brown horse running, then a man
followed after with a rope.

I could not believe what I was seeing.

When not in church now, on a Sunday morning,
I listen close for the dark horse running.
The hoofbeats like a recollection —
where are the dead, and who are the living?

And there is a fantasy:
a young girl loses her mother,
works after school helping a white lady
with housecleaning. Years later, as she knits
for her baby, she remembers the green backyard
where she helped wind yarn. The skein
fitted nicely around her hands. She learned
to knit in the green backyard.
The tulips. The roses. The daisies.

It had not been that lovely
then: her back hurt, her head ached,
some friends drove by in a car and did not
even notice her. *You don't remember the pain,*
a woman says suddenly to her in the
waiting room at the doctor's. *But suppose
they lied about her,* she wonders, pulling
at the yarn. *I have a fondness for the truth.
Suppose they forgot to ever tell it.*

Golf

It seems always two years ago
no matter which two years
I was a child
thinking I had grown.

Two years ago I was playing
solitaire in the frightening room.
At the center of each card
laid out on a brown table
was a pink ceramic lady.

Outdoors the snow
fell unpardonably.
What a child I was.

I could not speak intelligently
and found cards in the gutter.

And another memory.
My only time on the golf course
we whacked at balls.

I sat on the hill
watching the slope
slope down to the water.

I could not play golf automatically,
and having no other opportunity,
I never did. In the evening light,
no words for it — such a long slope —

to roll down it over
and over, the grass
long, thick, and cool.

What a child I was.
Other worlds were possible.
Other worlds were likely.

Child Hiding

The sun just now when it was hidden
was like a child in white behind a fish tank
and a breath of rain that was plummeting
nearly brushed my face. I must have moved

my head momentarily to protect my glasses,
then the cloudburst eased and came to the stop
it makes, eaves yet in the wet dim marbled way
they drip. I never saw such sunlight

in the yellow-green leaves of the cherry,
in its velvet black trunk. The lustrous
sun and the lustrous shades on the grass blades.

The sun was moving back of the wet white
clouds, and the color through or inside
everything was where and what it wanted to be,

and wanted to emerge from laughing. May every
one of us come running out glad. That prayer
depends on such a light, depends on life
going well, and right. So often we are saddened

like a child that leaves off hiding when he sees
it never mattered, his hiding place. To know
and to come away is what I would finally have to
learn, to suddenly grow chilly and close the door.

Pinks

PLANTING

Tonight is the night of the Last Supper.

As I cover the seeds with soil
the wind blows the packet off the rail.

All of it, all of it has fallen. Seeds,
leaves, earrings made of silver, shards of
glass, a gray cat that walked away fast
with his ears back. Fallen,
between these two close houses.

Is it an easier task to not be half-crazy,
to not poke around while I pick up the packet
for earrings blown off years ago in wind,

simpler not to let this wind catch in my hair,
as I stand lost in gravel in my bedroom slippers?

I think these pinks can never grow,
but later I sprinkle them tenderly with water.

And a striped fat tiger comes to the rail.
I spatter her gently then touch her
on the cheek. I have left her with a tear.

SPROUTING

How little or how much we will believe
stems out of the ground and keeps. Wings come there
to keep out of flood and stars wind up
circling through the leaves. Each doubt

curves out and flowers and must turn
to a useful or a dry seed. That is all
we can believe. When it is over, it never
shuts to a close like a leaf. How little
or how much we will believe.

ADDING

Statice into you, into the earth, like money.
Shredded paper, rivers of ribbons, confetti
from piñata, statice into you, big pot
that lost the jade. Guilty. But the crow
squawks, *planting, someone's planting*
someone's
pinks are sprouts and the jade's dead,
propped too badly during a hungry
cold musty and airless winter.
Statice into you, big pot that lost the jade,
statice into you, into the earth, like money.

HALLOOING

Hello, I halloo to the neighbor
during the empty threads
of his record. Uh, isn't it a little
high?
        By the way,
did you hear, tonight a comet
is passing by?
                Big mouth,
and in the background of earth
the striped cat is looking up

and eating, as striped cats look up
in the background
and keep eating.

VANISHING

Wings with a beak of wattling
and width between dark crosses on the air
width of light, let it nest there.
Who, who and what above the wasps
and hovering in what gutter
in the corner, what is there, then
wings gone, were hovering a moment,
are here hovering, or hovering elsewhere
and we are not the same about ourselves.

APPEARING

The bark like a rock makes a sack
or a man, his knees, and maybe a sack-
rock by him, a sack of sand or grass.
When I walk by him, every other tree
wheels saying, each, we are each a person.
We have staked our lives on being tree.
We have now and will always have
a right to be. And the bark is as strong
and beautiful as hand-carved stone.
Each made itself, its own
individual tree. Made itself, as though
each were made to make itself by someone.

White sun on bark
dark shade in the cracks running
over like water, darkness of water.
White sun on water, dark shade
like rocks or leafy shelter. Prefer

to follow the level path away from here
out of creation and into creating.
Prefer, prefer and make ahead
an arrow and fly there. Fly to
making over and over. Fly to
making, time after time. Fly
to making once or twice and then
once or twice again. Fly to making.

AUBADE—A DREAM

The last illumination
before the sun springs up
I can learn a single phrase
from an old Swedish book
before a heavy figure
comes from another room
I have the spelling right
The moon is not a slave
that ought to be a wine
heady as blackberry

BLOOMING

No better world.
All the situations
I ought to have understood
differently, rooms,
and in them, who I had to be,
the texture of the darkness
at the center of the cedar,
leaves that fell, the end
of time, it all storms around me
in the still August sun.

As though all luck
were in recognition of color
I take the yellow poppy
from the rubble in the alley
and a rare fly lights at my feet.
It is green like a jewel,
and there is no time
like the present
for the statice
to branch up, wake white, pansies
to face the face of the cat
in rapt devotion. The landlord
cordons off the porch
for the new steps, and briefly
it is a balcony, where
large and sturdy
rises one pink.

Horse Sense

Puyallup Fair
".. . a moral victory for lovable me."
—CHURCHY-LA-FEMME

In a shaft of sun from a huge roof near the flowers
and foreign foods I eat my egg sandwich with milk.
More coffee. More shadows. Two-hundred-twenty-pound squash
Goat pulls to climb the milk platform, her hooves
win! The pan fits under. White rabbit works his art
of *I Am Not Usual,* pink neon eyes in a barn

scented sweetly by racers and rollers. Barns
lightly littered with droppings, hay-clover flowers.
Please tuck in a corner the display of Fine Art,
mere ideas of sun, ideas in lines on a milk-
white ground, mere ideas about horse hooves
out of order as a two-hundred-twenty-pound squash

in the living room: nobody wants a squash
there instead of a hassock. I am in a real barn
I am city worn I need to hear the real hooves
of swine and goat and woolly lamb. And flowers—
each head has a halo. I can see a cow milked.
Tuck it modestly in a corner, the display of Fine Art.

But the flowers. The pansies and statice of *my* art
did not reach mammoth proportions like the squash—
but *a moral victory for lovable me* says pride's milk
continually, as tack creaks through the barn.
A sorrel labeled *Sweet & Sour* with a blue flower-
ribbon above him looks at me & whickers. His hooves

want to pound grass below us. His hooves
pound the stall. He sees me, he says to me, *Thou Art.*
I believe. But I see myself falling in flowers
while he laughs and runs off turns tight at a squash
like he turns round the barrels. The floor of the barn
has thick sawdust where I stumble. To the sworl of milk

in dapples (gentle-giant rumps), in cream-colored milk-
tooth baby small in straw near the draft hooves
in the shadow where I started—the cold draft horse barn.
Splendor of the row brushed to lustrous art,
let me stand very peaceful with enormous horses and squashes
let me know that the source is a jungle of white flowers—

oh giant milky flowers that make the air thick... oh milk
that feeds the horses, squashes, giant... that pumps to the hooves...
oh cloud-white art of milk pervading the barns...

Like Swallows
At the Pilings of the Ferry

The crows have flown over
the shoulder of the island
making faraway cries.

And it is very quiet
at the weather-beaten store
that will not open.

In there a banana
has started to speckle.
From a dry bench in the dusty porch

underneath drying fuchsias,
at last I stand, and others
are coming straight at me.

She with a baby,
three dogs following
through water

a dark young man
a pale city couple
a white-haired truck driver

who wheels down beer cases
two vans and a car full
of school kids from Etonville.

We circle, we circle,
we try the door,
ignoring each other,

we walk onto the long
fishing dock, or up
to the blackberry brambles.

We are absent to each other.
A chalk-white gull flies close
and small. Mallards swim under

like monks in a row. I see
no shadow appearing, reappearing
above them in their sky.

Once I wondered
why they never collide,
the swallows. That was when

I was that certain,
swinging giddy in the circle
of my own errand.

Destinations

The smell of cooked ground turkey is as heavy
as the sandalwood incense I burn by the sink
where the dishes dry in the rack. A wealthy time
superimposes indecision on an unclear, fattened
image, hazy in light from the white evening
window. The plants may blossom before summer ends.

I walk in the evening, leave the harsh
shouts of the crowd of children or the stereo
blaring downstairs or the sounds passing cars
make at the corner stop sign. The dark eases
some of this, when wind rises and the ash leaves
sigh, but in the heat of the early evening
I walk past the houses where their sprinklers
wash the lawns in that slow repetition.

I cannot bring myself to go nowhere. I cannot
visit the crowded park where the sounds of people
multiply. I need a destination. The last time
I walked I left twenty-four exposures, over a year
in pictures, at the Safeway. There is a book at
the library. And I need to borrow a saw from home.

My father insists on wrapping it in newspaper
like a fish for me while I look at my pictures
with my mother. Sometimes I forget
my friend who stands pale on my porch
visiting from California, or the poets at the
wintry marina, or one who looks up laughing,
sun brightening her deck and the freeway below it
and the friend who came back from Montana
and her daughter petting the cat. (The cat had
watched mole holes in the garden, then vanished
the next day and was never heard from again.)

My father wraps the saw and says he bought that
before I was born, when they lived at the old place.
When he was in England, some sergeants got him
to make a scabbard for their axes, and a scabbard
for another axe at the hospital. Pharmacists
were jacks of all trades then, I suppose.

The book from the library keeps me up all weekend.
It is about Christina, in England after World War One,
where her husband died in a PBS serial I saw
three times and kept the music on my tape recorder.

At the end all her plans have turned out badly. She
rushes a fence in the sunset. The whole story suddenly ends.
I cry for an hour. I have not cried like that,
over anything, for a long, long time.

Exposures

Rain batters the window. Indoors all is still.
Behind the glass door of the cupboard—a camera
covered with dust. For fifty years inside it

they have waited on the small wooden porch.
They have stood very still in their black suits
by the curved slat bench and the trellis,

they have seriously and long held their peace
with their overexposed white faces. She has waited
there for fifty years, her legs still slender,

her new hat shaped like Napoleon's. She turns
on her hassock. She turns her face, her ribbon,
her cut black hair as though she turns from the piano.

The newspaper and her uncle's shirt-sleeves—
white as history's snow. All the men are seated
at the sun-bathed kitchen table. A hand moves

momentarily from one man's knee to his chair.
For fifty years the camera has concealed the error.
Her hand takes the film from the camera back—
a nut from a shell when she wants it whole.

The Gord Family Orchestra

Four brothers on the wall
in shades of gray framed in brown.
Charles is sitting down among the others.
He has fathered five sons and a daughter.
Like saints in a niche within an arch
at the foot of half-a-stair
above the grass-green shade, glass
painted with roses on a cloth-covered table
by a Swedish Bible.

Carl works with electrics. He repairs
radios in a workshop in the garage.
Gilbert has installed a buzzer
that calls them from the bedrooms to the kitchen.
Upstairs in the morning
the buzzer wakes them, one, then
another, and they walk downstairs

to the smell of coffee on a wood stove
of pale green enamel. Boxes beside it are filled
with kindling, blocks from the stacks in the basement.
Men bring the wood and leave it at the top
of the driveway. Each week a man brings ice
when he sees the signal—a card in the window.
He carries it with tongs up the long back stair.

My mother walks downstairs.
She faces her piano in the corner,
brown and upright, sheets of music
at eye level, the revolving stool
adjusted to her height.

She types. She has fine
penmanship. She stands, riding

the streetcar home from work that night.
Her aunt works at the flour mill.
Her mother irons that day on the mangle
they have bought her, she presses the bodies
of the shirts out flat.
They make dinner for a crowd
at the oilcloth on the kitchen table.

Then the Gord Family Orchestra
(the brother who fixes radios carrying
his banjo, my mother with a briefcase filled with
sheet music, the plant worker with
his accordion, and Gilbert who has placed
his drums in back) goes down to the garage.
They carefully back the car

up the steep incline past the basement under
the high kitchen windows, past the porch light
that shines across the dark front grass,
between the lilac and the holly where is sprawled
a cord of wood covered with tarpaulin,
down the steep hill toward the railroad track
and the dock beyond that, and across town

to the Valhalla Temple, where the varnished floor will creak
beneath the feet of the Swedes, the dancing will lift
up lightly through the polkas, through the hambos,
then when the orchestra pounds an end to a whirling schottisch
they will stamp on the floor until the floorboards shudder.

Late, the car in the garage, they carry their shoes
up the long back stair. The little brother
stumbles and begins to imitate a drunk,
they laugh and are suddenly
lining their shoes across the kitchen floor.
In the dawn their mother finds
the line of stiff and stitched scuffed leather.

Old Garden

I walked down through my uncle's garden today,
looked deafly at the horsetail forest,
saw the black slug lift its horns under the blossoming
salmonberry. I thought I heard a rat
in the raspberry bushes suddenly
running away under the tilting clothesline mast.
And as I passed back under the porch to the steps,
I happened to look in the basement window —
the gray sink taps, and tucked behind, a broken
piece of china, painted with apricot oranges,
pale transparent raspberries, and I thought
how well it was arranged, this art of home.

My uncle is ill, my mother brings him meals
on Saturday. I came to steal lilacs
and look at what was there, what slips away.
As they grow old I can realize
not much from looking, but that we were children.
Behind that overgrowth of blackberries
is a woodlot. A dogwood's flowers hang over

where we walked in the eye of the sunlight
through leaves. Once I followed my sister
to the end of the blackberry path
and there at a strange house a dog barked at us
in yellow light I cannot say for sure was fear.
And the small white rose my grandma's sister planted.
It is old. The new tunnels through.

There is a lot of change, my mother says. Exchange.
A piece of ground for a horsetail, a piece of ground
exchanged for a sapling that can rush up

when my uncle is ill and become a tree.
A cut of road through the blackberry bramble.
A child can see what is wild can be taken,
what is worked on is possessed.
And does not interfere. Waits to do that
until grown. A child does not learn what is yours
is the possessor. Takes itself back at the last
until retaken. And am I no child anymore?
I was too moved by the garden to speak.

A Poem about My Father

His mother picked a switch up
and whipped him back the hill
when he wandered down to the tracks.

She died when he was six.
That was all he could recall.

Morality, look at the shell.
All soft parts, it kept working.
Morality. It made and made.

*

Living so close to the lake, the sunlight
glittering drew him down. We drove near
the site of the house, and the lake lost light
as late afternoon slanted. I remember
dark trunks and shadows of leaves
the lake behind them unwelcoming.
When they thought he should swim, they
threw him in. One brother
died in World War One, one went to the East,
one was Uncle Fred, who made his living
as a salesman and the owner of a five-and-ten.
They lifted my small father off the ground
and threw him in where it was deep.
The cold lake was a lake he swam out of.

*

We stopped to see his sister,
who raised him. She lived on a farm
near Sedro Woolley. He wore the dark suit
he wore working at the drugstore. After
he ran away to work she lost her sight.
She married a fundamentalist.

They lived in sun in a dark house in her
sightlessness. In my astigmatism
a dark house, a heavy woman,
the scent of pigs heavy in the air.
It tastes of vines where pea pods fattened.
We ate from the open pods.

*

He told us his grandfather lived in the woods
and visited leading a goat by a rope.
The rope ends must have frayed and haloed
in sunlight when great-grandfather stepped
out of the dark woods.

*

When he worked for Standard Oil
he tried to photograph the seagulls
from a deck, but their wings blurred.
He tried to catch what was impossible.
He worked in the galley. In Mexico—
into some seaport then out of it—
they met some nameless revolution.

*

At the fish trap rains knocked fish and men
out of knowing sea from sky,
but the salmon, each one a muscle that is bowing,
bowing to catch the element and sweep
away from vacancy, lost it,
lay gasping in a swarm.
In the grease of the kitchen he cooked
for the men, while the rains nearly
washed them away.

*

He showed up at the logging camp hungry.
The foreman gave him money to buy boots.
He walked to town for them over stones
on the railroad tracks. Above him sky,
around him the mountains of Montana.
He walked all day, and for that day
he was not paid.

*

While they were raising the gargoyles,
while they erected the building,
in front of Suzzallo Library
the Reserve Officers Training Corps
drilled in formation.

*

We heard this over biscuits
in my mother's breakfast nook, the night
black at the windows.

And the story of the man
who during World War Two in England
poured gravy over his pie.

He told us, *Life is hard.*

Swedish Fish

Like jewels in a box they shine
from the counter at the grocery.
Our jewels are like candy, like ideas.
Like icicles and like iced horses
trotting on icy stony ground.

Far away in a stony country
with a sea I have never seen,
yellow-green trees float in cloudy sun
in trembling summers like candy fish
that dream the winters in frozen water
beneath the surface of stony snow.
There. Swimming there.

Four paper cartons strewn with holly.
A flap at each top, a thin metal handle.
I filled them with sweets
and walnut fudge. A fish in each,
pikes from the candy store.

My sister praised dime-store goldfish
netted from an aquarium and held there
butting the edge until you poured them
into a bowl. Comets or fantails,
orange and sometimes speckled
with white. There, swimming there.

But that evening my cousins praised
Chinese food, steaming from metal
cooking pots in kitchens of Chinese
restaurants, ladled into cartons
to carry home in the car. Fish. Swimming there.

And on the edge of her chair in lamplight,
my mother praised peanut butter,
ladled from a barrel downtown
when she was a girl. She looked for it
whenever she opened a jar. Grainy
and oily. Fish, swimming there, on top of

the candy. Not able to self-transfigure,
or to reidentify. I could praise nothing.
Let me praise that evening. I carried
a carton to his house where I hung it
over the mailbox hoop. And stood helplessly
praising the rusting hoop that received it.
Praising the thin metal handle
by which it hung. Let me praise
the gray sky too, the way it darkened
above the trees on my way home.

V

Lessons

The rind is thick as an old unabridged
you open up deep to reach meaning.

The sections are the same, some
close, some cleft, and definite.

You want each part
to be cool, and sweet, and wet.

When you leave the library
it has been raining. The swallows
are playing in the grass.

You are a counter in their game.
You move at a predictable rate.
You and a tree they may fly between
until you two meet. Remember

that they dart in the morning sun
near the ash leaves
near the window.

And the orange when it separates
has arches like their wings.

You want each part
to be cool, and sweet, and wet.
One word must be swallow. Swallow.

Money

The rich who are not wealthy,
what can they bear of money?
What can they stand of dollars,
of it bloody quietly spent,
the body painlessly bleeding?

A mirror was the beginning,
and every mirror after
encircled the same brooding eyes,
made them its own possession.
And then a face there by mine.
May Life happen.

The hand has two sides now;
the leafless wood in the palm,
the bamboo under-finger;
the tanned top, knuckled river
skin loose on bone
grown delicious by use.

What Heaven knew of gold's color
they put first into the sun,
let some run over a river,
and buried some.
The same coin has two sides.
May we turn it over and over.

Sleep in May

Morning, a cloud of sun swallows bat through.
Charmed, they work at catching hanging buzzing
things that are too slow in the trees. That
like me cannot wake. And the telephone rings.
I cannot reach it. It rings again. A policeman
asks me to the policemen's circus and he says
he is sorry to wake me. I was not asleep, I say.
And I am not lying. I cannot remember.
The Hawaiian is my neighbor. His car is stalled.
He is outside with the hood up, black-haired
and floral in our calm plain spring. Only
the swallows work, quickly circling. I sleep.
All this has happened before. Sleep I cannot stop
that comes to me without surprise or panic.
Mornings slow and long made up of clouds of sleep.
The sun the part in my hair, my ear unreality.
And then a blessed wasp buzzes in to terrify me!

Women Who Take, and Men Who Give

Snow for two mornings. The first night,
a creaking in the storm-broken trees,
a squeaking cradle
that kept me at the open window
looking through the black for the scraping branch.

It sounds like a woman
calling a cat, a treble
prrt, prrt in the street,
but it is wood on wood,
a hanging-empty bough.

Then snow, first over my eyes
in a vision, far off through a vision of trees.
Then dust on the ground.

Gray and deep and real
from the pearl sky
an intimate wind kisses the crosses
dropping the laces away
hesitation in wet air
then a drift into the ground,
then undistinguishable.

All day I am out, but you know
I am afraid of the dark, that then
I will be in. I want to talk.

When the sun goes down you call.
You have been forgotten.
You were not on the list
when you reached the hospital for testing.

white threads hospitals are woven from
steel instruments, a steady ability
that cannot and does not
reassure

I cannot tell you of the silence,
of the snow I make my bed from

but stand I will, half-senseless and uncertain
at the window, saying spinning visions
now angel him, now live him well.

Earlier

See through the trees in a field of light,
you can follow the distance the pony's neck
stretches down to the grass. The sun makes a lamp
of the barn. Out there it seems good.
The bus vibrates.

Earlier. Last year. I was thinking of death:
how much better to sleep? Night that black crow
takes you under her wing? The pony

lowers its head, and I am suddenly
elsewhere, and earlier, than that,
elsewhere when the bus goes past the bay
where the tugboat makes froth I can see through
to elsewhere, and deeper, and earlier.

At dawn I step out, lift my eyes to the trees.
The people at the bus stop follow me. They work
in a workshop. They see that hammering
woodpecker I do not see. They say Sunday
we set our clocks back. One must have been wrong,
the others say no, no, four o'clock. Earlier.

The pony that sleeps out in the field
does not know that this first bus comes earlier.
That I wish it could come earlier than that:
in every culture something went wrong.
I want to set it back before the Fall of Man,
before the flood, the burning library at Alexandria,
before the Crucifixion, before Hitler,
Hiroshima, before Vietnam, before war and heartache,

before my latest error in judgment, before
the latest cruel thing I said. Earlier.

But I wake only early, when the light slips in
to the window curtains and wakes
the birds, the pony, the grass, the sundial...

Gray Area

Outside a young black man drives by.
I am suddenly blond. I am Scandinavian.
How dark they are.

Fancy—sweet, the sense of us
always checking to make sure
no maniac of our own persuasion
has eliminated
them, them always watching
to be sure
the Scandinavians are still
left.

Sweet if there were no hunger
anywhere, no trouble
in their old country.

All of a sudden
the middle of a pleasant afternoon
I have not heard a crow.

I stand and look through all
the budding branches that are
large at the stem, cross-hatched far
to the edges. And far
stand two black forms
in the gray area. How do I know
after three months every day
away, these are not the only ones?

A gray head working in her garden.

2.

Did the war
that made our parents' lives
make us aware
all of a kind of someone
could be done away with?

Or have we known that forever?

Here is another question, one
that is larger:

Is the black bird the brimming pulse
of hate inside my brain?
Is my idea, which is my instinct
impulse?

Is there a morality in question?
the black bird and the black person

Who can tell me?
Is this sweet or cruel?

3.

Again, how Scandinavian I am.
Let me make up a story.

But the story is a dream too sweet for words.
I know the name of America's
racial history: trouble.

But:
the woman touches
her child and says Finland.
The woman touches
their child and says Africa.

The woman will imagine
no trouble.
She wants for her children
no trouble.

She wants to change the name
slowly
to:
a bad dream that ended
sweet dreams
now

Her Porch Light

shining means someone is there
but that might not be true.

I keep saying the stars mean everyone matters.
But how much tonight can I be wrong about?

The stars are not alive unless I own them.
The rose and cherry do not belong to me.

And her porch light reflects on me.
I am a fool to stay with night and day

in fragments, I see no hope in love.
When a moth lights for a moment

on my hand how necessary it is that it stay
in its own body, stay a moth

because I will touch it if it comes
as a cat or a man and brush its feathers away.

Her porch light shines on anything that stands
there in the yard with the wind in it. The roses

are gone. The cherries are gone. The bush
and the tree are alive. I think for a moment

those stars are alive, and then
one bright one moves.

I think a small plane, I have come to pray now

to be right about even such a small thing.

Then I hear a small jet and I am wrong
and it is going nowhere I am aware of.

Mountaintop

Weeds deliquesced and flowered from dusty ground,
brick-red, butter-yellow, and blades
knifed the sky in places, blooming too.
Flowers like daisies, purple flowers like lupine.
I looked down and caressed. We crowded through
the blades of leaves and a grouse shot up
whacking its wings against the colored air.
In the chill of my shadow, the eye of a grasshopper
burned up like fire. In the chill of my shadow
the leaves shaped like stars grew white as ice.

The tram is for such vision in summer, and for
the crazy chatter going down, and for these
rapid eyes, the shot of sight to the tongue.
For we pass by rocks so like Titan extremities
so like sandstone soles and toes and the hands
of rock that caress them, that we become small.

Shelter

I had bread rising in a warm oven.
I dusted what was left of the flour
off of and into my jeans
and went downstairs and opened the door
for mail. I found
a woodpecker dead on the threshold.
A hawthorn berry beside it.

I brought a box of white plastic packing chips
down and petted it on the feathers then
picked it up in my hand,
the feathers warm, the body light
and cold. It fit exactly
into the hollow I made for it.
The hawthorn berry beside it.

I left it on the kitchen table.

I thought of it looking
for shelter, coming only into the porch
to a nest at the corner the door made
where it met the jamb, the whole of it
carved with leaves and varnished
in the summer when the landlord repainted.
Or flying into the shapes of blowing trees
in the door window.

And I thought of three tame trees where I walk
that had brushed my head and filled it with dreams
that fell in the summer
to be cut for firewood.

I found a broken shovel
that sits at the side of the house
and buried it bare in a break in the clouds.
Beside the house, under the hawthorn.
The hawthorn berry beside it.

As I walked back to the stairs
the box fell open, and chips
shaped like esses and ees
flurried out on the wind like flakes of snow.

And I took the bread out of the oven,
baked now. An oatmeal loaf.

Laura Jensen lives in Tacoma and teaches at Tacoma Community College. She has received grants from the Literature Program of the NEA, the Washington State Arts Commission, and the Ingram Merrill Foundation. SHELTER is her third full-length collection of poetry.